IGNITE YOUR SALES POWER!

MINDFULNESS SKILLS FOR SALES PROFESSIONALS

also by
JOY RAINS

Meditation Illuminated:
Simple Ways to Manage Your Busy Mind

IGNITE YOUR SALES POWER!

*MINDFULNESS SKILLS
FOR SALES PROFESSIONALS*

JOY RAINS

Whole Earth Press®
Bethesda, MD

Whole Earth Press
A Division of Key Seminars, Inc.
P.O. Box 34816
Bethesda, MD 20817

Publisher's Cataloging-in-Publication data

Names: Rains, Joy, author.
Title: Ignite your sales power!
mindfulness skills for sales professionals / Joy Rains.
Description: Bethesda, MD: Whole Earth Press, 2017.
Identifiers: ISBN 978-0-9886699-1-8 | LCCN 2017914032
Subjects: LCSH Selling. | Mindfulness (Psychology) | Success in
business. | Mind and body. | Performance--Psychological aspects. |
BISAC BUSINESS & ECONOMICS / Sales & Selling / General
Classification: LCC HF5438.25 .R347 2017 | DDC 658.85--dc23

Editing by Barbara E. Kahl
Cover and interior design by David Moratto

Printed in the United States of America

The recommendations and meditations contained in this book are not intended as medical advice and may not be suitable for everyone. Please check with your health care practitioner before implementing any changes in your lifestyle habits. Meditation should not be done while operating a vehicle, device, or equipment of any kind or while engaged in any other activity that requires your attention. Neither the author nor the publisher shall be liable or responsible for any loss or damage allegedly arising from any information contained herein.

For Dad,
who pointed the way
to a sales career

CONTENTS

Preface . . . . *ix*

Introduction . . . . *xi*

I. FUEL

Chapter 1: **MEDITATION** *3*

Chapter 2: **IMAGINATION** *25*

II. AIR

Chapter 3: **CONCENTRATION** *51*

Chapter 4: **CONSIDERATION** *61*

III. SPARK

Chapter 5: **DETERMINATION** *77*

Epilogue *89*

Appendix: 18 Ways to Develop Your Power of Awareness . . . *91*

A Final Thought *129*

Acknowledgments *131*

＊

PREFACE

BOTH MY FATHER and my grandfather were professional salesmen, so selling is part of my DNA. When I was in high school, I landed a part-time telemarketing job and began a long sales career, following in their footsteps.

After college, I earned my living as a traveling saleswoman, selling optical products to wholesalers. I moved on to selling computer products to the U.S. government, then telephone systems to commercial accounts, and finally print and online advertising to businesses.

When I began my sales career, I noticed that some sales reps rose to the top like heavy cream and others sank to the bottom like heavy weights. I wanted to understand this disparity, so that I could be one of the salespeople who rose.

In the early 1990s, learning to meditate taught me how to become mindful — and how to develop the enormous power of awareness. Roadblocks became easier to navigate. Opportunities became easier to recognize. Business poured in. Sales flourished.

I was so excited about the benefits of mindfulness and meditation that I wrote a book for beginning meditators, *Meditation Illuminated: Simple Ways to Manage Your Busy Mind*. (You'll find some excerpts from it in Chapter 1.)

Since mindfulness was key to my business success, I decided to write this book on mindfulness for sales professionals. You'll find ideas, lessons, and techniques that can help you rise to the top. My intent is to help you boost your business — and ignite your sales power.

Hope you enjoy!

INTRODUCTION

THE POWER OF AWARENESS

ONE COLD MORNING before the days of electric cars, I was miffed that my car wouldn't start. My husband turned to me and matter-of-factly stated, "You need three elements for ignition: fuel, air, and spark."

Now you can discover elements to ignite your sales power. Within these pages, you'll find a framework of three parts: *Fuel, Air*, and *Spark*. You'll learn how to build your power of awareness with mindfulness skills — and how to apply these lessons to best practices for sales.

Here's a summary of each section:

I. FUEL
MANAGING YOUR THOUGHTS

Your thoughts are fuel for your mind and for your actions in the world.

Learn how to:

- Navigate a path to the sale with meditation.
- Realize your potential with your imagination.

II. AIR
GIVING SPACE TO YOUR CUSTOMERS

Rather than immediately filling the air with the benefits of your product, fill it with curiosity — and compassion for your customers.

Learn how to:

- Identify customers' needs and challenges with concentration.
- Establish a loyal customer base with consideration.

III. SPARK
GENERATING ENERGY TO DO YOUR JOB

My father used to tell me that sales is the worst paid job for those who don't work hard — and the best paid job for those who do!

Learn how to:

- Stay motivated with your determination.

I recommend picking and choosing the techniques that resonate with you. The more engaged you are in this process, the more successful you'll be.

At the end of each chapter, you'll find an Action Plan with suggestions for techniques and practices to try, ways to evaluate their effectiveness, and recommendations for moving forward with them. You'll find an additional Action Plan within the body of Chapter 2.

The Appendix contains eighteen ideas for practices to try. You can try a new practice each day, or skip around and choose those you like. Note the ones that resonate with you and try to integrate them into your sales activities.

I hope you discover the practices that are right for you, so you can ignite your sales power!

※

※

I
FUEL

MANAGING YOUR THOUGHTS

*Your thoughts are fuel for your mind
and for your actions in the world.*

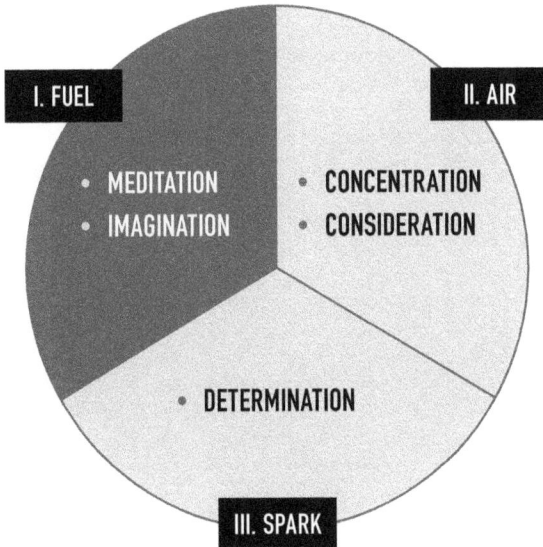

✳

Chapter 1

MEDITATION

NAVIGATE A PATH TO THE SALE

MEDITATION IS A practice of training the mind to develop present moment awareness. This awareness is called mindfulness. Mindfulness allows you to become aware of both your internal experiences, such as your thoughts — and your external experiences, such as what your customer is communicating.

In this chapter, you'll learn how awareness of your internal experiences can help you recognize thoughts that could impede your sales efforts. You'll learn how to meditate — so you can release thoughts that don't serve you, clear your mind, and navigate a path to the sale.

To start, let's take a look at the nature of thoughts, and how awareness of your thoughts can improve your results.

THOUGHTS AND AWARENESS

It's widely reported that the average person generates anywhere from 50,000 to 70,000 thoughts per day. Thoughts may range from bigger issues (*Should I make a career change now?*) to thoughts about smaller issues (*Should I eat lunch before or after my appointment?*) to judgments of liking or not liking (*I love this new product!*) to regrets about the past or worries about the future (*I'll never overcome her objection!*).

Thoughts often happen at lightning-fast speed, either with the same thoughts repeatedly cycling through the mind, or with the mind jumping from one random thought to another. Consider, for example, a sales professional meeting with a customer. As there's a pause in the conversation, her mind wanders. If you could listen to her thoughts, you might hear: *I hope I can close this deal. Maybe then I'll win the trip to Hawaii! Better get to the gym, so I look good in my bathing suit. Darn! I ate too much cake last night — but hey, it was my birthday. I can't believe how old I'm getting!*

Thoughts like these can become obstacles to the sale. Rather than paying attention to her customer, this sales rep is allowing her thoughts to pull her away from the present moment. If she's distracted, even just momentarily, it might be at the moment her customer says, "If your software will save us time, I think my managers would be interested." She could miss this important buying signal and the opportunity to understand her customer's needs — not a good formula for sales success.

Meeting prospects and customers with a clear mind can be challenging. After all, just as it's the nature of the heart to beat, it's the nature of the mind to think. I call the mental content that cycles through the mind "Stuff," which is an acronym for:

Stories
Thoughts
Urges
Frustrations
Feelings

Stuff serves an important function, since it helps you navigate through life. Yet, you may not even realize this Stuff is present. It can fade to the background of the mind, but it's still there, influencing your behavior.

Try this: Pause for one minute. Notice what's going on in your mind — your STUFF.

Some people are surprised by the amount of STUFF they notice during this one-minute exercise. Others don't notice much of anything at all. The point of the exercise is to be aware of your experience; there's no right or wrong.

Awareness will allow you to make a conscious choice about how to manage your STUFF, so it doesn't distract you. You'll learn how to develop awareness with meditation later in this chapter.

THOUGHTS AND JUDGMENTS

Thoughts can also become obstacles when they're in the form of negative judgments. If a potential customer looks unhappy, do you interpret that as meaning he's not interested in your product or service? If you hear the economy is in a slump, do you tell yourself a story that your sales will collapse, as well?

Consider an example from my experience.

It's the monthly meeting of the National Association of Professional Saleswomen, sometime in the 1990s. The room is filled with 100 saleswomen, waiting to learn how to make a telephone cold call. I'm presenting.

"First, let's break the habit of saying 'how are you' when the prospect answers the phone. It sounds canned and inauthentic."

"Take the envelope from under your chair. There's a balloon inside with 'how are you' printed on it. Blow up the balloon and tie it in a knot."

"Now, let's break the habit!" I stomp on my balloon. One hundred women follow suit and the air fills with sounds of balloons breaking.

People are laughing and having a grand time, except for one woman, an esteemed colleague in the audience, scowling and shaking her head in disapproval. Rather than noticing everyone who's having fun, my eyes are drawn to her like a magnet. The voice in my head says, *She hates your presentation.*

She's an expert in this field and her opinion matters. My heart sank.

Afterwards, when everyone had filed out of the room, she was waiting to talk. She said, "I loved your message, but that noise, the noise of the balloons breaking was so loud, it reminded me of my difficult childhood, growing up in a violent neighborhood."

This woman's reaction had nothing to do me. I created a negative story around her response, giving the story a meaning that had more to do with my insecurities than anything else. Awareness would have enabled me to realize: *This woman is scowling and I don't know why.* Instead, I reacted to a story that turned out to be false.

Consider this: Have you ever told yourself a story that led to a lost sale? How else could you have responded? Take a moment to reflect.

Your judgments directly affect your responses. What's your response if a customer says "no"? If you realize you're treating a customer's negative response as a permanent roadblock, consider looking deeper to see if there's another path to the sale.

As ancient Greek philosopher Epictetus wrote, "We cannot choose our external circumstances, but we can always choose how we respond to them." Developing your power of awareness will allow you to respond to life's events *consciously*, rather than react to them *unconsciously*.

THE PRACTICE OF MEDITATION

A proven way to build your awareness is through the practice of meditation. Meditation helps you clear your mind, as you learn to release distracting thoughts and negative judgments.

Meditation is a practice of noticing. You don't try to stop thinking; rather, you allow your STUFF (Stories, Thoughts, Urges, Frustrations, Feelings) to surface and then let it pass, without judgment or internal comment. You practice noticing your experience in the present moment, observing your STUFF as if you are witnessing it.

The awareness you develop during meditation can make a profound difference in your sales results. In addition to practicing at a regular time, I recommend taking a few minutes to meditate and clear your mind before contacting customers. A clear mind will help you recognize opportunities and navigate roadblocks. As you become aware of the present moment, you may be more likely to notice your customers' body language, such as posture changes that signal likes or dislikes. You may become more aware of your customers' audio cues, such as shifts in voice inflection. You may become more aware of subtle, underlying issues as you listen closely to your customers' words. These observations will give you insight and help guide your responses.

Imagine setting your goals aside before contacting customers, clearing your mind, and approaching your sales call with *present moment awareness* — a sense of being completely grounded in the here and now. As you meet with your customer, instead of your mind being in "drive" to reach your goals, your mind will be in "neutral" — allowing you to pay attention to your customer's wants and needs, understand objections, and recognize buying signals. Keeping your focus on the present moment will help you navigate a path to the sale.

HOW TO MEDITATE

I recommend choosing a regular place to meditate, so you can practice building your power of awareness. Sit on a chair or floor cushion in a quiet room. Start with 2–3 minutes, setting a timer if needed. As you become used to practicing, gradually increase your time to 15–20 minutes a day if your schedule allows. If you're short on time, try to meditate for just a few minutes to maintain a daily routine.

Here are steps to follow:

1. Start by sitting up straight, without being rigid. Keep your spine aligned with your head and neck. Gently close your eyes. Try to release any physical tension, keeping your body relaxed — but your mind alert.

2. Choose an anchor — a neutral focal point that doesn't stimulate your mind. Commonly used anchors are: your breath; your body; a word repeated silently, such as *peace;* a sound you listen to, such as ocean waves; or an object to hold, such as a smooth stone.

3. Rest your attention on your anchor. Whenever your mind wanders, gently refocus on your anchor. For beginners, this may be as often as every second or two. Although many people think the practice of meditation involves stopping all thoughts and feelings, this is not so. Expect that thoughts and feelings will continue to arise.

4. Accept your wandering mind. Meditation is a practice of returning to your experience in the present moment. Again and again and again. *Notice* when your attention wanders, and then *return* your attention to your anchor. The intent of meditation isn't to suppress thoughts and feelings. Consider anything that draws attention away from your anchor to be like a cloud passing, or like a boat floating by as you watch from the riverbank. Allow it to pass without judgment and gently refocus on your anchor.

5. Continue gently refocusing on your anchor for the rest of your practice time. This process is key, since it exercises your mind's "muscle." Just as the repeated practice of doing abdominal crunches can build your core strength, the repeated practice of noticing dis-

tractions and returning to your anchor can build your power of awareness. The practice of shifting your attention to a neutral focal point (your anchor) is like shifting your mind out of "drive" and letting it rest in "neutral." Each time you refocus on your anchor, you're training your mind to let go of distracting thoughts.

Meditation is a simple practice, but it can be challenging. As stated earlier, people often have the best success by starting with brief periods of regular practice time and gradually increasing the length of time spent meditating as they become used to practicing.

WHEN TO MEDITATE

You can meditate almost anytime. (Note: Don't meditate when driving or performing another task that requires your full attention.) It's important to practice when it works best for your schedule. Meditating for a few minutes is preferable to not meditating at all.

Many people find practicing first thing in the morning works best, before they get busy with the day. It's helpful to schedule meditation practice to coincide with an activity you do regularly, such as brushing your teeth in the morning.

In addition to regularly scheduled practice time, consider meditating before contacting customers, taking time to release any distracting thoughts. For instance, if the roads were congested on the way to meet a customer, you may be feeling rattled, or if the CEO of your customer's company is expected at the meeting, you may be anxious. Try a *Simple Breath Meditation* or a *Body Awareness Meditation*, as described later in this chapter. You may want to set a timer on your phone to keep you on schedule.

WHERE TO MEDITATE

I suggest creating a dedicated meditation place — a place to regularly practice developing your power of awareness. Over time, you may find your mind begin to quiet down by simply entering your dedicated place. Meditation places can even be portable — for example, a meditation cushion that's used in different settings. An entire room in your home could be devoted to meditation — or just a corner of a room. One meditator carved out a small space next to the dryer in her basement laundry room by installing a sliding translucent screen. Another transformed a bedroom corner into a private space by using a sheer curtain as a divider. Another uses a favorite chair in the living room.

A meditation place should include a dedicated place to sit, such as a chair or meditation cushion. Some people also like to include inspirational items, such as books of short readings (for before or after your practice), meditation beads, candles, or music.

You can practice meditation almost anywhere. If you meditate before a sales call, you may want to find an out-of-the-way park bench or a quiet corner in an office building lobby. You could even meditate in your car — once it's parked!

SIMPLE MEDITATION PRACTICES TO TRY

You can choose from the following practices — and also find audio meditations posted on my website, www.joyrains.com.

BODY AWARENESS MEDITATION

A stress response can take place both in your mind and in your body. What happens when a prospect says "no"? Do you tense up? If you're anxious about a sales presentation, do you hold stress in your body? Imagine coming into awareness of physical tension and releasing it. You can practice body awareness almost anywhere, anytime.

Use this as a stand-alone practice or as a starting point for other meditations. Begin with your head and move your awareness downward to one muscle group at a time. Alternatively, start with your feet and move your awareness upward to one muscle group at a time. As much as you can, try to relax each muscle group before moving on to the next one.

You can release muscular tension with your imagination, visualizing your in-breath surrounding the tension and your out-breath gently releasing it. Or, imagine the tension becoming warmer and melting away. Take as much time as needed. If any tense areas won't release, see if you can accept them as they are.

You can also tighten each muscle for a few seconds and then relax it, to differentiate between a tensed muscle and a relaxed muscle. Be gentle and don't strain.

Throughout this process be aware of your body and how it feels. Allow your spine to support you, and allow the seat and ground beneath you to support you. Release any muscles not needed to support you. Keep your body relaxed but your mind alert. Try to develop a muscle memory of what it feels like to relax.

SIMPLE BREATH MEDITATION

Start by sitting up straight, without being rigid. Keep your spine aligned with your head and neck. Gently close your eyes. Try to release any physical tension, keeping your body relaxed and your mind alert. Rest your attention on the pace of your breathing, without changing anything; simply notice. You might notice the coolness of the air as you inhale and its warmth as you exhale, or you might notice the rising and falling of your chest. You could even silently say "rising" with each inhale, and "falling" with each exhale. Each time your attention wanders, gently refocus on your breath.

SMOOTH STONE MEDITATION

Choose a smooth stone that fits in your hand. Start by sitting up straight, without being rigid. Keep your spine aligned with your head and neck. Gently close your eyes. Try to release any physical tension, keeping your body relaxed and your mind alert. Then, shift your attention to the stone in your hand, noticing its various characteristics, including: its weight, temperature, shape, texture, and size. Each time your attention wanders, gently refocus on your stone.

You can also keep your meditation stone in your pocket to remind you of an intention, for example, being relaxed or staying focused.

MORE WAYS TO PRACTICE MINDFULNESS

You can also cultivate mindfulness by considering your activities to be meditative practices, as if the activity itself is your anchor. For example, consider integrating brief mindfulness breaks into your daily routine, such as pausing for a moment and noticing two full breaths, washing your hands and noticing the feel of the soap and water, or eating a meal with full awareness of the textures and flavors of your food.

Another simple way to integrate mindfulness into your life is with a walking meditation. As you walk, gently bring your attention to the soles of your feet as they touch the ground. Any time your attention wanders, gently bring it back to your feet. You can practice this for a few steps, a few miles — or any distance you'd like. Consider using a walking meditation as you transition from one place to another. World-renowned meditation teacher Thich Nhat Hanh says to "be aware of the contact between your feet and the Earth."

MORE BENEFITS OF MEDITATION

One significant health benefit of meditation is reduced stress. Since mindfulness helps you experience life in the "here and now," you may notice tension that you hadn't noticed before. For example, you might realize that your breathing is shallow or your muscles are tense — or, that you're adding to your stress by imagining negative scenarios. Becoming aware of tension can help you release it. Try a *Body Awareness Meditation* to help you release physical tension or a *Simple Breath Meditation* to help you release mental tension.

Many scientific studies point to significant mental and physical health benefits of regular meditation. For more information on the health benefits, see the National Library of Medicine's website at www.ncbi.nlm.nih.gov/pubmed/ and search "meditation."

ACTION PLAN

❋

EXERCISE

Pause for a couple of minutes before a sales call. Choose an anchor to use. Gently rest your attention on your anchor. Release your STUFF each time you notice it, and return your awareness to your anchor.

Alternatively, listen to an audio meditation before contacting your customer. You can find recordings of varying lengths on www.joyrains.com.

As you walk to your customer's office, rest your attention on the soles of your feet as they touch the ground. When you talk to your customer, see if you can maintain present moment awareness. Any time you notice your thoughts wandering, gently bring them back to your customer, as if your customer is your anchor.

EVALUATE

After you meet with your customer, rate the following statements on a scale of 1–5, with 1 strongly disagreeing and 5 strongly agreeing.

✳ I was able to release physical tension prior to my meeting. *1-2-3-4-5*

✳ I was able to clear my mind prior to my meeting. *1-2-3-4-5*

✳ I was able to focus on my customer. *1-2-3-4-5*

Based on these ratings, what will you do again — or do differently — on your next sales call?

MOVING FORWARD

What practice or practices would you like to integrate into your life? Possibilities include:

✳ Meditating at a regular time each day.

✳ Setting up a regular meditation place at home.

✳ Taking a moment to clear your mind before contacting customers.

✳ Trying to become aware of physical tension and releasing it.

✳ Evaluating your quality of awareness after sales calls.

✳ Using a walking meditation when transitioning from one place to another, noticing the soles of your feet as they touch the ground.

✳ Listening to guided audio meditations, found by searching "guided meditation" online or found on www.joyrains.com.

✳

Learning to direct your attention is one of the most powerful ways to navigate a path to the sale.

❋

CHAPTER 2

IMAGINATION

REALIZE YOUR POTENTIAL

Y OUR IMAGINATION HAS a tremendous amount of power. You can change your outcomes by using your imagination to change your beliefs about reality. Since the brain treats imagery the same as it would treat real-life action, new behaviors can be "ingrained" in your mind simply by engaging your imagination.

When you couple the power of your imagination with the power of awareness, you can intentionally plant positive thoughts in your mind. In this chapter, you'll learn how to create your vision of success and realize your potential by activating your imagination through:

- Words, using positive statements called **affirmations**.
- Images, picturing your goals with **visualization**.

Of course this only works if what you imagine is within the realm of possibility. If you're a sixty-year-old man with lower back problems, and you visualize an outcome where you're the star player of a pro-football team, it's unlikely you'll actually realize your vision.

REALIZE YOUR POTENTIAL WITH AFFIRMATIONS

The technique of using affirmations is a powerful way to use your imagination when you *aren't* with your customer — to help optimize results when you *are* with your customer. Affirmations are written or spoken statements that describe your goals as if they're already happening.

For instance, you could use the following affirmations to help you find new prospects: *I easily find customers who are eager to do business with me; My prospecting activities create bridges to a future pool of customers; I approach prospecting with a sense of expectation and adventure.*

Note your affirmations on index cards, on your computer, tablet, or cell phone, in a journal — or anywhere that you're likely to see them. Once you have your affirmations written, repeat them silently or aloud, while imagining them to be true.

TIPS FOR USING AFFIRMATIONS

If you've never used affirmations before, using them may seem awkward at first. If this is the case, putting that awkwardness aside and mustering up a belief in the power of the affirmation will bring the best results. The more you believe the affirmations to be true, the more effective they'll be.

PRESENT AND POSITIVE

- Write the affirmation in the present tense, as if it's already true. Affirm *I listen closely to my customers* instead of *I will listen closely to my customers*.
- Say what you *are doing* in the statement, rather than what you *are not doing*. Affirm *I make efficient use of my selling time* instead of *I do not waste my selling time*. Avoid negative words such as "not" or "none."
- If you notice internal resistance to an affirmation, try a "willing to" affirmation first. For example, *I reach out to new prospects every day* can be changed to *I am willing to reach out to new prospects every day*. Once you accept the affirmation as true, use the affirmation without adding "willing to."

PERSPECTIVE

- Use first, second, and third person. *I, Jessie, easily imagine achieving my goals. You, Jessie, easily imagine achieving your goals. Jessie easily imagines achieving her goals.* People's beliefs are affected by external sources, so it's helpful to use the affirmation from another's viewpoint in addition to your own perspective.
- Keep your affirmations related to your actions, not someone else's actions. For example, affirm *I'm aware of new opportunities all around me*, instead of *new customers contact me every week*.
- Keep affirmations realistic, affirming for goals or ways of being that are achievable.

PRACTICE

- Write each of your affirmations ten to twenty times daily, record and listen to them, or read them aloud or silently. Try to develop a daily habit, using the affirmations first thing in the morning, before bedtime, or throughout the day. You can also use affirmations before a sales call.
- Use no more than three to five different affirmations a day, either using the same affirmations every day or using different ones, according to your preference.

- Keep your affirmations where you'll see them. Post them on your bathroom mirror, on your refrigerator, or on a nightstand. Carry them on an index card or electronic device, and refer to them regularly.

AFFIRMATIONS TO TRY

Here are affirmations you can try, listed under various categories: Goal Setting, Focus and Relaxation, Prospecting, Listening, Value and Confidence, Features and Benefits, Objections, Closing the Sale, and Perseverance. Some are repeated under multiple headings. Only use statements that resonate with you.

GOAL SETTING
- I easily imagine achieving my goals.
- Deep within myself, I am determined to meet my goals.
- Every time I reach a goal, I set a new goal.
- I can envision my goals as if they're already true.
- I have a clear picture of my goals.
- I review my goals regularly.
- No matter what happens on the outside, my sense of purpose remains strong.

FOCUS AND RELAXATION

- ○ I allow my body to relax before contacting customers.
- ○ I'm able to maintain a regular pace for my breathing.
- ○ I easily recall muscle memories of being relaxed.
- ○ I'm able to remain centered and balanced even in high-stress situations.
- ○ No matter what's going on outside me, I remain focused.
- ○ I'm relaxed and alert during my sales calls.
- ○ I easily calm my mind before contacting my customers.
- ○ I take a couple minutes to relax and release tension before contacting customers.
- ○ When I'm with my customer I'm able to stay focused on the "here and now."
- ○ I'm able to clear my mind before meeting with customers.

PROSPECTING

- ○ I easily find customers who are eager to do business with me.
- ○ I am confident in my abilities to generate new business.
- ○ I anticipate that prospects and customers will be interested in my product or service.
- ○ My prospecting activities create bridges to future pools of customers.

- I approach prospecting with a sense of expectation and adventure.
- I'm aware of new opportunities all around me.
- I'm in the habit of regularly contacting my prospects.
- I prospect with the long-term picture in mind.
- I genuinely care about my prospect's needs.
- My product or service is of great value to my prospects and customers.
- I approach my sales territory with a sense of abundance and success.
- I realize that success can take patience as I sow the seeds of future sales.
- I realize that my continued efforts will bring the fruits of my labor.

LISTENING

- I listen closely to what my customers say.
- I listen for problems that I can help solve.
- I ask open-ended questions to help discover my customers' needs.
- I paraphrase what my customers say to make sure I understand them.
- When my customers speak, I'm able to focus on what they're saying.

- I encourage my customers to talk about their needs.
- The more my customers speak about their needs, the more I understand them.
- I have a deep respect for my customers, and it shows in the way I listen to them.
- I have a genuine interest in my customers as people.
- Before I talk about my product or service, I make sure I understand my customers' needs.
- Listening to my customers is the bridge to understanding them.
- I practice sharpening my listening skills with family and friends.
- Listening is a way of life for me.
- Before I talk about my product or service, I encourage my customers to talk about their needs.
- I ask open-ended questions to discover what's important to my customers.

VALUE AND CONFIDENCE

- I am confident in the value of my product or service.
- I believe my product or service will benefit my prospect or customer.
- I relate the value of my product or service as it pertains to my customers' needs.

- I like who I am.
- I believe in myself and my abilities.
- I believe in the value of my product and service.
- I easily communicate with my customers.
- I'm happy to see my customers, and I anticipate that they're happy to see me.
- I'm able to focus on my customers and their needs.
- I enjoy helping my customers solve their problems.
- I value my time and my customers' time.
- I have a strong belief in the value of my product or service.
- I am the bridge between my product or service and my customers.
- I have tremendous value to offer customers and prospects.
- I trust in my ability to communicate value to prospects and customers.

FEATURES AND BENEFITS

- I clearly communicate solutions to my prospects and customers.
- Once I understand my customers' needs, I relate features and benefits to match their needs.
- I always follow a feature with a benefit.
- I say the words "so that" after a feature, *so that* I'm led into relating a benefit.

- I communicate the features and benefits of my product clearly and concisely.
- I speak in simple terms that are easily understood.
- I present the features and benefits of my product and service with enthusiasm and conviction.
- I have a clear understanding of the features and benefits of my products or services.

OBJECTIONS

- When I hear "no," I realize it can mean *not right now* or *tell me more*.
- When I meet an objection, I consider it as an invitation to find out more.
- When I hear an objection, I find out if there are other objections, or if that's the only one.
- I have a clear understanding of potential objections and how to meet them.
- When I hear an objection, I see it as an opportunity to ask my customer more questions.
- I expect to meet objections as part of my job, and I look at them as requests for more information.
- When I hear objections, my determination allows me to move beyond them.
- I meet objections with an open attitude.

- I repeat objections back to my customers to make sure I clearly understand their concerns.
- I show my customers I have an understanding of their objections.

CLOSING THE SALE

- I know when to ask my customer to make a decision.
- I pay attention to my customer's interest throughout the selling process.
- I know which questions to ask to close the sale.
- I recognize my prospects' buying signals and know when to close.
- The sales process often unfolds so naturally that the sale seems to close itself.
- I close with frequency and with confidence.
- After I ask for the sale, I always stop talking and wait for my customer to speak.

PERSEVERANCE

- My belief in the value of my product or service helps me persevere.
- When I hear "no," I realize it's about something other than me.
- When I hear "no," I ask for more information.

○ Each "no" I hear brings me closer to a "yes."

○ The more people I ask, the more I hear "yes."

○ Part of my job is to ask — again and again.

○ I find multiple reasons to stay in contact with my prospects and customers.

○ I trust that there's a pool of customers interested in the benefits of my product or service.

○ I trust that there's a pool of customers interested in doing business with me.

○ No matter how I feel, I'm able to take actions to fulfill my goals.

○ I stay positive on the inside no matter what happens on the outside.

Choose affirmations from these lists — or create your own, following the suggestions in *Tips for Using Affirmations*, described earlier in this chapter. Once you've tried your affirmations, referring to the Action Plan at the end of the chapter can help you integrate them into your life.

Consider that today's thoughts create tomorrow's results.

ACTION PLAN

EXERCISE

*Practice using a few different affirmations
that resonate with you.*

EVALUATE

*After you've practiced using your affirmations,
rate the following statements on a scale of **1–5**, with
1 strongly disagreeing and **5** strongly agreeing.*

* I was able to identify or create affirmations that resonate with me. *1-2-3-4-5*
* I can easily imagine the affirmations as if they're true. *1-2-3-4-5*
* I believe using affirmations will create positive outcomes in my life. *1-2-3-4-5*

*Based on these ratings, what will you do again —
or do differently — when using affirmations?*

MOVING FORWARD

What practice or practices will you integrate into your life as a result of reading this chapter? Possibilities include:

☀ Writing and reviewing affirmations regularly.

☀ Looking at written affirmations every day, while imagining them to be true.

☀ Trying a "willing to" affirmation if you feel resistance to a particular affirmation.

☀ Displaying affirmations where you're likely to see them.

☀ Recording affirmations and listening to them at night.

☀ Using affirmations before contacting customers.

☀ Continually adding to affirmations as your goals change.

☀

Consider this:

*Since it's the nature
of the mind to think,
you may as well
choose thoughts
that serve you.*

REALIZE YOUR POTENTIAL WITH VISUALIZATION

Another powerful way to use your imagination to realize your potential is with visualization, a practice of envisioning the outcome you want as if it's already happening. As Napoleon Hill, author of *Think and Grow Rich* said, "Whatever the mind can conceive and believe, it can achieve." When you imagine something as if it's real, your mind and body often respond accordingly — as if what you imagined actually *is* a reality.

Sports players use visualization all the time. They envision hitting that home run, getting that perfect golf shot, or making that touchdown. They've mentally rehearsed the game-winning play so many times, the odds are favorable that they'll achieve what they believe.

A colleague of mine, Steve Watson, is a motivational speaker and retired pro-football player who was a wide receiver for the Denver Broncos. Steve found visualization to be one of the most effective practices to ignite his game. Steve gave me permission to share his process:

> The visualization began at the beginning of the week as we would watch game tape of the next opponent. The tape was broken down into different

categories so that we could identify exactly how the opponent would play us in that situation. Teams play different defenses and techniques at different times during the game. My job was to be able to anticipate how they would play against me during those situations and try to counter what I thought they would do against me. This physical counter that I was planning to do against them was simulated or practiced during the week using several variations that I thought were possible answers to beat them. It is difficult to identify what you are really going to do until it is time to do it. By identifying and practicing the moves during the week you can create a situation "where you are never surprised by what you see in the game." That is the concept behind the visualization. When I lay down and put the towel over my face before the game in the locker room I literally felt myself working those techniques during the course of the week during practice. I was able to see myself scoring at that time during the game. This was the concept of "playing the game before I played the game." When the QB called the play in the game you knew if it had a chance when you jogged to the line of scrimmage. Then it was time to put the practice into play. I would take a deep breath and "drop into the zone." It's at that moment all the noise, all the distractions, everything in the outside world is silenced. I am in a moment of complete concentration as I work the technique that I practiced that week to beat the opponent.

Steve visualized positive future outcomes, while also calling on memories of past successes to propel him forward. As he said, he "played the game before he played the game." With his imagination, he created a blueprint for a winning career in the National Football League.

Visualization can help you reach your goals, whether you're a professional football player or a professional salesperson.

HOW TO PRACTICE VISUALIZATION

You can practice visualization anytime — for instance, before getting out of bed in the morning, before going to sleep at night, or during the day.

To practice, find a quiet place to sit or lie down, then close your eyes and spend some time relaxing your body. You may want to refer to the *Body Awareness Meditation* in Chapter 1 as a reminder of how to release physical tension. After focusing on your body, shift your focus to your mind, envisioning the results you want as if they're already happening. The more specific, the better. The more senses you engage, the better. Visualize as many different aspects as you can, including what you see, hear, smell, taste, and feel. You can even imagine yourself as if you're witnessing your behavior from someone else's perspective.

Be sure to take your time with the visualization. It's most effective if you feel you've actually lived it, so it becomes second nature to you.

Some people find it difficult to visualize a particular outcome if they don't have a memory to draw upon. If this is the case, try to imagine someone else who's achieved the outcome you want. See if you can visualize it from their perspective, and imagine being in their shoes. For instance, a brand new sales rep might find it challenging to visualize herself closing a sale if she's never closed a sale before. In this instance, she could imagine how she'd feel if she were her sales manager, who's had years of sales experience.

She could also visualize scenarios that represent success, such as skillfully prospecting through LinkedIn or receiving the Top Salesperson award. The more she imagines

she's a top producer, the more her behaviors — and beliefs
— will line up with this vision.

Keys to powerful visualization are:

- Being in a relaxed state.
- Repeating your visualization often.
- Involving your emotions.
- Imagining what you experience with your five senses.
- Keeping your visualization within the realm of possibility.

CREATING YOUR VISUALIZATION

Answering the following questions in detail will help create
a starting point for your visualization for sales success.

Who is your ideal customer?
- Company type, size, and location.
- The title or position of most of your customers.
- The need or needs your customers have in common.

What do you offer?
- Scope of offerings.
- Unique offerings.
- Corporate and personal support available to customers.

Where can you find prospective customers?
- Referrals.
- Networking and social media.
- Other sources.

When will activities take place?
- Prospecting.
- Customer meetings.
- Follow-up.

Why should your customer buy from you?
- Immediate benefits related to customer needs.
- Long-term benefits related to customer needs.
- Benefits of purchasing from you and your company.

Try this: You can practice reaching out to customers by envisioning yourself contacting them, whether by phone, email, or other means. Imagine a large pool of customers who would be happy to hear from you. Perhaps a customer has been too busy to get back to you and would welcome your call, or maybe you haven't yet contacted a prospective customer who is struggling with a problem that you can solve.

No matter what the circumstance, it's vital that you're continually visible to decision-makers and buyers. Pause for a moment and consider that you're the link between the customer and your product or service. Imagine picking up the phone and making the call or making contact through other means. Put aside any images of negative outcomes. See if you can just focus on the task at hand, which is to make contact and move the sales process forward.

Remember, your imagination has a tremendous amount of power — and what you believe, you can achieve.

———————

"Take up one idea. Make that one idea your life—think of it, dream of it, live on that idea. Let the brain, muscles, nerves, every part of your body, be full of that idea, and just leave every other idea alone. This is the way to success."

— Swami Vivekananda, 19th century sage

ACTION PLAN

EXERCISE
Set aside time this week to practice using a visualization.

EVALUATE
Are there particular situations where imagination can be an important tool for you?
How can you use your imagination to improve your outcomes?

MOVING FORWARD
What practice or practices will you integrate into your life as a result of reading this chapter? Possibilities include:

* Practicing using visualization regularly.
* Practicing short visualizations before sales calls.
* Using visualizations to meet new challenges.
* Using visualizations to expand your potential.
* Regularly reviewing your visualizations.

❋

II
AIR

GIVING SPACE TO YOUR CUSTOMERS
*Rather than immediately filling the air
with the benefits of your product, fill it with
curiosity and compassion for your customer.*

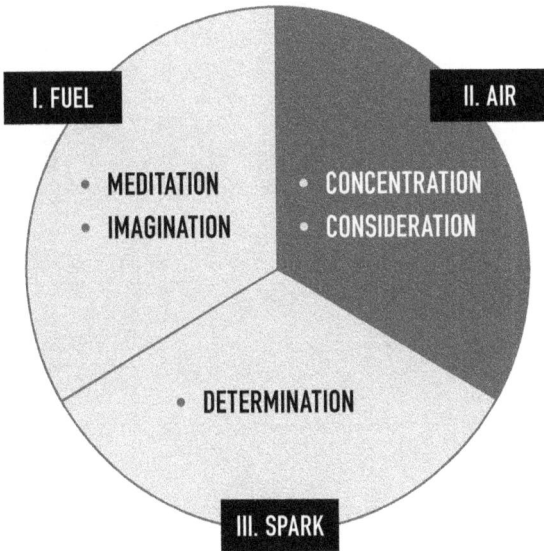

I. FUEL
- MEDITATION
- IMAGINATION

II. AIR
- CONCENTRATION
- CONSIDERATION

- DETERMINATION

III. SPARK

※

Chapter 3

CONCENTRATION

~≈~

IDENTIFY CUSTOMERS'
NEEDS AND CHALLENGES

THE PREVIOUS CHAPTERS focused on using mindfulness to help you notice your internal experience (your STUFF) as you released distracting thoughts, cleared your mind, and imagined success.

Now, you'll learn about the importance of becoming aware of your external experience, for example, what your customer is communicating. This will help you identify which questions to ask and ultimately, which benefits to present.

The first step in developing this awareness is to allow space for customers to communicate their needs. As they talk, concentrate on both verbal and non-verbal cues, paying attention to customers' words, voice inflections, and body language.

Paying close attention can be challenging, especially since the mind can process words at a rate of approximately 500 words per minute, but people talk at a rate of approximately 150 words per minute. Perhaps you've had the experience of listening to a customer and realizing your attention has been pulled away by distracting thoughts.

Consider the customer to be your focal point; each time your STUFF distracts you, bring your attention back to your customer. You can use the following three mindful listening tools to help you focus on customers, encourage them to talk, and identify their needs and challenges.

1. QUESTIONS

Some salespeople fall into the trap of spewing the features and benefits of their products, while not understanding what the customer wants. This dynamic was shown in a well-known sales training video, where comedian John Cleese played a travel agent who didn't ask the right questions to identify the customers' needs. A couple walked into the travel agency and said they'd like to go on a vacation. Cleese's immediate response was, "How about Australia?" The couple declined. Cleese said, "How about Belgium?" The couple declined again. "Canada?" "No."

"Denmark?" "No." "England?" "No." The scene sped forward as Cleese worked his way through the alphabet and finally landed on Zurich. The couple still said, "No."

Cleese could have narrowed down this couple's preferences by asking open-ended questions to uncover their needs.

Make a list of questions to ask your customer. Continually add to and revise your list.

Here are some questions to get you started:

○ What is your decision-making process?
○ Who else is involved in purchasing decisions besides yourself?
○ What is your timeframe?
○ What is your budget?
○ When does your new fiscal year start?
○ What is most important to you?
○ What is your vision for the best solution?
○ What is your vision for success?
○ When will this fit into your schedule?
○ What challenges are you facing?
○ How can I help you?

2. RESPONSES

After asking a question, stay engaged as your customer responds. Use *minimal encouragers*, which are verbal and non-verbal responses that don't interrupt the speaker. Examples are: saying, "I see," "mmm-hmm," or nodding your head. Minimal encouragers give your customer cues that you're listening and encourage the customer to talk about needs, wants, and visions for solutions. You can also pick up on the last word the customer says with a lilt to your voice. For instance, if the customer says, "I need to get my inventory more organized," simply responding, "More organized?" will likely encourage the customer to elaborate. It's important not to interrupt or finish the customer's sentences, since that would take the focus away from the speaker.

Once your customer pauses, wait an extra second or two before speaking. This lull in the conversation not only gives you a chance to collect your thoughts, it also gives your customers space to continue talking if they have more to say.

Paraphrasing what your customers say will also help you identify needs. Here's how I learned about this important skill: While in college, I worked on a telephone crisis intervention hotline. During my training for the job, the supervisor's instruction to "repeat what the callers say back to them" was confusing. I said, "You want me to repeat what the callers say back to them? Wouldn't that be awkward?" The supervisor looked at me with a twinkle in her eye. "You think it would be awkward to repeat what the callers say back to them?" I nodded emphatically. "Yes, I do! (pause) Oooh. Now I get it."

When you repeat your customer's messages back, it creates understanding and shows the customer you're listening. It also leaves room for a customer to say, "I didn't exactly mean that, what I really meant was this." You can either paraphrase the customer's words throughout your conversation, or when your customer is finished answering your questions, by saying, "Just so I can make sure I understand ...," and then summarize what you just heard. Of course, it's fine to let the customer know you're going to jot down a few notes, so you can remember key points. People appreciate it when others aim for clear communication.

3. SILENCE

Here's another important lesson I learned while working as a telephone counselor: *It's not like radio, where you can't have dead air time. It's all right to have some silence.*

Some salespeople are uncomfortable with silence, whether in person or on the phone. Perhaps you've experienced salespeople who, when finally reaching a customer by phone, are afraid to stop talking, since it will leave room for the customer to say, "I'm not interested."

Silence is OK. In some sales situations it's actually desirable. Many sales training classes teach the value of not talking after asking for the sale, since you could be interrupting the customer's train of thought.

I learned this lesson the hard way when I was a new sales rep selling optical products. As a young woman meeting with an optician thirty years my senior, I felt intimidated, though I tried to appear confident. While showing him a line of designer sunglasses, I asked, "Which ones would you like?" He chose seven pairs, which wasn't enough to meet the minimum order of ten, so I suggested he get an extra pair of his favorite three styles to meet the minimum. This optician didn't appreciate my suggestion. He slammed my sample case shut, exclaiming, "That means I'd have $300 tied up in this!"

Although I hadn't planned on allowing for silence, I was so frightened by his response that I couldn't move or speak. I was unintentionally abiding by the sales rule, *once you ask for the order, zip the lip.* After what seemed like hours, but probably was just a few minutes, he re-opened the sample case and said, "I'll take two each of these styles." The value of silence. The value of allowing space.

Here's another time when silence worked out favorably. Again, it wasn't this sales rep's intention to be silent. As she told it to me, an employment agency sent her to interview for a sales position. She described the interviewer as having words tumbling from his mouth for 45 minutes non-stop. She hoped for a pause where she could jump in and present her qualifications, but no luck; she barely got a word in edgewise before the interview was over. As she sat in the coffee shop planning her next move, her phone rang. "Hi! It's Sarah from the employment agency. They want to hire you. They said you were the best candidate they talked to!"

* * *

People love to have someone take an interest in what they say. The more you listen, the more you can learn, and the more you learn, the more likely it is you'll uncover a need you can fulfill with your product or service.

ACTION PLAN

❋

EXERCISE
Practice using mindful listening tools.

EVALUATE
After meeting with your customers, note the effectiveness of the mindful listening skills you used.

MOVING FORWARD
How will you use these skills in the future?
Possibilities include:

❋ Making a list of questions to ask customers.
❋ Continually updating your list.
❋ Practicing using mindful listening skills with customers, friends, and family members.
❋ Practicing incorporating silence into your sales calls.
❋ Visualizing using mindful listening skills.

"You can make more friends in two months by becoming interested in other people than you can in two years by trying to get other people interested in you."

— Dale Carnegie, author, *How to Win Friends and Influence People*

⁂

Chapter 4

CONSIDERATION

ESTABLISH A LOYAL CUSTOMER BASE

ONSIDER THE SALESPEOPLE you've encountered. Have you ever dealt with someone who didn't allow space to find out about your needs and talked "at" you? If you remember someone like this, it's likely because they didn't make you feel valued or understood. People prefer to buy from those who understand their needs.

In this chapter, you'll learn to develop empathy for customers by practicing compassion meditations. Empathy is the ability to understand, be aware of, and be sensitive to the thoughts and feelings of another. Showing compassion and empathy for your customers will help build trust, loyalty, and strong customer relations.

Scientific studies point to the ability of compassion meditations to enhance the capacity for empathy. For more information on these studies, refer to the National Library of Medicine's website at www.ncbi.nlm.nih.gov/pubmed/ and search "compassion meditation."

DEVELOPING EMPATHY

I'll always remember this car shopping experience: As I walked across the car dealer's parking lot, my foot landed on a wad of chewing gum that was baking in the hot summer sun. When I stepped forward, multiple strands of gum stretched from the bottom of my shoe to the pavement. I scraped, rubbed, and struggled to remove it. While I was leaning against a car, standing on one leg, and cleaning the bottom of my shoe, the car salesman approached. He was completely oblivious to my dilemma. "How ya'll doing? What type car you wanna buy today, ma'am?"

If this car salesman had been empathetic, he would have helped me to a chair where I could clean my shoe before he began his sales pitch. Instead, he talked AT me — and lost the sale.

Take a moment to consider how you like to be treated by salespeople. Most people, if faced with stepping on a wad of chewing gum, would appreciate someone who says, "Have a seat over here and let me help you."

When you treat customers well — or not well, for that matter — they're likely to share their experience with others. A happy customer tells a friend; an unhappy customer tells the world.

As poet Maya Angelou said, "People will forget what you said, people will forget what you did, but people will never forget how you made them feel."

BRING KINDNESS TO ALL YOU ENCOUNTER

Here's a time where a sales rep I was working with changed his attitude toward a challenging, long-time customer. If it weren't for the fact that the customer spent thousands of dollars a month on his product, he wouldn't have spent time calling on her.

Nancy managed to find something wrong with every order. The rep couldn't find a way to think of her with compassion. He realized he was caught up in his stories about Nancy — how he thought she was so difficult, how it was so hard to please her, and how he felt stressed every time he met with her.

Just as Nancy focused on the negative side of doing business with his company, he focused on the negative side of doing business with Nancy. Kidding with this rep, I offered him an emergency "generic good thought" to apply to Nancy: *Her exhale feeds the plants.* All kidding aside, I recommended that he try to shift his thinking about her, and also consider that she directly or indirectly provides him with his commission.

I suggested that he bring a sense of compassion and kindness to Nancy. Instead of looking at his customer as a difficult person, he could try to recognize her as a struggling human being just like him — a human being with needs, likes, and dislikes. Maybe she has a mortgage she's struggling to pay, or a kid who needs braces, or a boyfriend who stays out too late with his buddies. Although he doesn't know her exact circumstances, he can still treat her with compassion.

I also suggested he practice bringing this sense of compassion to all his customers, not just the challenging ones. I reminded him that his customer is not an "it," not a means to his ends, and not a number to check off on his sales report.

I told him about Martin Buber, an Austrian philosopher born in the latter part of the 19th century. Buber's claim to fame was his book *Ich und Du*, usually translated as *I and Thou*. His premise was that people think of humanity in one of two ways. The first way is to think of the other person as an "It," or a person to be used, and the second way is to think of the other person as "Thou," or a person that's the same as you — there's no separation; you both are one. The Dalai Lama reflected this sort of thinking when he said, "We are all the same."

The sales rep told me the next time he called on Nancy, he made a conscious effort to set his judgments aside. He noticed he was anticipating that she'd be difficult even before he got to her office — and his body tensed up as a result. He decided to spend a few minutes in his car practicing a *Body Awareness Meditation* where he tensed and relaxed each muscle group to release physical tension. He imagined himself going into Nancy's office and looking at her with eyes of compassion.

When he actually walked into her office, he noticed a picture of her family and he thought of his own family — which reminded him that "we are all the same." He felt a shift to a more positive attitude and realized that bringing compassion to his prospects and customers was a practice he'd like to continue.

HOW TO PRACTICE BEING COMPASSIONATE

If you'd like to practice developing empathy and being compassionate, here's one way: practice compassion meditations. This type of meditation may feel awkward if you've never practiced it before, but believing in the intent of the meditation can help cultivate a true sense of compassion for others.

To start, sit down in a quiet place, either at home, in your office, or in your parked car before a sales call. Spend a few minutes noticing your body and releasing as much tension as possible. Then, silently recite these phrases to yourself:

May I be held in compassion.
May I be free.
May I be at peace.

If these phrases didn't resonate with you, change the phrases to ones that do. Other commonly used phrases are: *May I be well, May I be safe, May I be healthy,* or *May I be happy.* It's important to state the phrases in the positive, since it's more powerful to use a positive statement than a negative statement. For example, use the phrase *May I be safe* as opposed to *May I not encounter harm.* Begin the series of phrases with a focus on yourself; unless you have kind feelings toward yourself, it's difficult to have kind feelings toward another.

If you have trouble directing kind feelings to yourself, imagine someone directing these feelings toward you, envisioning a time when you felt warmth sent your way from a parent, child, friend, teacher, pet, or even by a stranger with a friendly smile. You could also imagine receiving kindness from the subject in a photo or painting who offers a warm gaze outward into the world.

Spend a few minutes or longer reciting these phrases and directing kindness toward yourself. Imagine what it feels like to receive compassion. Take a couple of minutes to become aware of any images, sensations, or feelings in your mind and body.

Next, spend time directing kindness to someone in your life you care for deeply and silently recite the phrases:

May you be held in compassion.
May you be free.
May you be at peace.

Again, if any of these phrases don't resonate with you, change the phrases to those that do.

Imagine what it feels like to send compassion. Take

a couple of minutes to become aware of any images, sensations, or feelings in your mind and body. Spend a few minutes or longer reciting these phrases and directing kindness toward the person you care for.

Next, recite the same phrases imagining someone you feel neutral about. This could be anyone you encounter in your life but don't really know, even the barista at the local coffee shop. (Although you may feel anything but neutral when you're handed a delicious hot drink!) Again, notice your experience while keeping this person in mind.

Now for the hard part, which is to direct these phrases to someone who is challenging for you. Directing kindness to this person doesn't mean that you like or accept their behavior; rather, it means you hold this person in compassion despite the behavior. The idea is to accept your negative thoughts, rather than push them away — and to be aware of your experience as you practice this meditation.

Finally, you can end the meditation by bringing a sense of compassion to your community, your country, and the whole world, as you recite the phrases:

May we be held in compassion.
May we be free.
May we be at peace.

Consider practicing this meditation before contacting a challenging customer. You may find that the sense of resistance you've had before will dissipate.

Here's another short meditation that can also help you develop a caring attitude as you wish your customer well.

Say to yourself:
May I be happy.
May I be healthy.
May I live a life of ease.

And then keeping your customer in mind:
May you be happy.
May you be healthy.
May you live a life of ease.

And then keeping both of you in mind and inviting anyone else in:
May we be happy.
May we be healthy.
May we each live a life of ease.

Here's one more compassion meditation. It's designed to start with compassion for your own needs, then your customers' needs, and finally the needs of the two of you together:

> *May I care about myself.*
> *May I care about my needs.*
> *May I see myself with eyes of compassion.*

> *May I care about my customers.*
> *May I care about their needs.*
> *May I see them with eyes of compassion.*

> *May I care about our time together.*
> *May I care about our needs.*
> *May I see our meeting with eyes of compassion.*

Your sales efforts are not about you; they're about serving your prospects and customers. Bring all your focus to them as if they're close friends, with a sense of compassion and caring — and a sense of curiosity about their needs. People like to buy from those who care about them. Make your customer the most important person in the world and believe in your ability to do business together.

ACTION PLAN

❋

EXERCISE

Try a compassion meditation before your sales calls.

EVALUATE

Were you able to cultivate compassion
for your customer by using these meditations?
Note any observations.

MOVING FORWARD

How will you develop compassion for your customers
moving forward? Possibilities include:

❋ Continuing to practice compassion meditations before your sales calls.

❋ Practicing a compassion meditation before contacting a challenging customer.

❋ Practicing a compassion meditation upon rising in the morning or before going to bed at night.

❋ Practicing a compassion meditation that you've written yourself.

❋ Searching online for "compassion meditations" to find additional ways to use them.

❋ Imagining treating yourself with compassion.

❋ Imagining treating customers, colleagues, friends, and family members with compassion.

❋ Noticing how you feel when practicing compassion meditations and trying to tap into this feeling when you're with clients.

❋

Truly having a desire to understand your clients' needs will show your compassion.

*

III
SPARK

GENERATING ENERGY TO DO YOUR JOB

"There is a force within
that gives you life. Seek that."

— Rumi, 13th century poet.

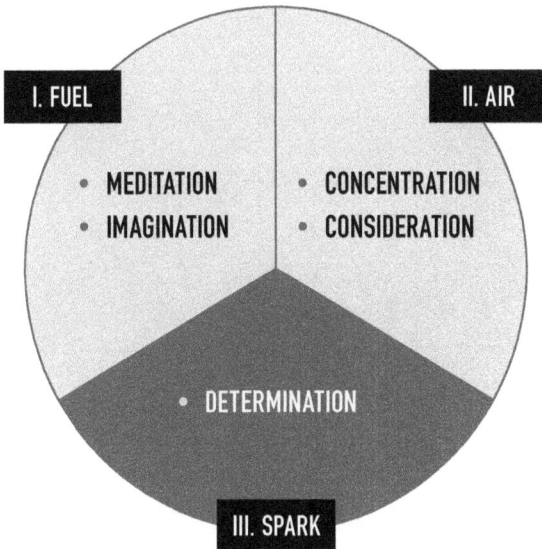

I. FUEL
- MEDITATION
- IMAGINATION

II. AIR
- CONCENTRATION
- CONSIDERATION

- DETERMINATION

III. SPARK

※

Chapter 5

DETERMINATION

STAY MOTIVATED

WITHIN YOU, YOU have the answers to what makes you tick. Even if you already know what motivates you, consider trying the techniques in this chapter to help you discover additional factors. Developing awareness of your motivators will remind you *why* you're doing *what* you're doing — and help keep you determined through challenging times and accelerate your success in good times.

Motivation is what gives you incentive and drive, and determination is the decision to keep going. In this chapter, you'll learn to identify what drives you by practicing an introspection meditation, using guided imagery, and using the right-hand/left-hand method of journaling.

* * *

A college friend of mine was one of the most determined people I've ever known. She graduated from high school at age 16, graduated from college at age 19, and completed her MBA by the time she was 21. She landed a sales job in the banking industry, trying to win business from the CFOs of large corporations. This was in the days before email, so she worked diligently to reach her prospects by phone. One executive never returned her calls. She decided to use a methodical approach, and she began calling him regularly — every Wednesday at 3 p.m. He still didn't take her calls, but she kept calling for a full year, every Wednesday at 3:00.

She ran the risk of alienating the prospect by calling so often, but she figured she had nothing to lose. This type of persistence might not fit every salesperson's style, and it's important to do what works for you.

Finally, after 52 weeks of calling him, she mailed him a one-year anniversary card — one year since she had started calling him! He finally called her back. And she landed a huge, lucrative contract.

Her ability to tap into her motivation for achievement helped her win this account. Notable psychologist, David Clarence McClelland, claimed motivation is based on the unconscious needs for achievement, affiliation, or power.

Identifying your unconscious needs can help you stay focused on your sales efforts.

Consider this: Can you recall a time when you were so driven that nothing could stop you? Whether this was a sales situation or a different circumstance, see if you can identify some of the factors that propelled you forward.

Here are three techniques to help you develop awareness of your motivational factors.

1. INTROSPECTION MEDITATION: WHAT IS MY MOTIVATION?

This technique invites you to sit with the question, "What is my motivation?" Rather than choosing an answer ahead of time, see if you get clarity on your answer during the meditation.

Start by sitting up straight, without being rigid. Keep your spine aligned with your head and neck. Gently close your eyes. Try to release any physical tension, keeping your body relaxed but your mind alert.

You may want to relax your body as described in Chapter 1: Begin with your head and move your awareness downward to one muscle group at a time. Alternatively, start with your feet and move your awareness upward to one muscle group at a time. As much as you can, try to relax each muscle group before moving on to the next one. You can release muscular tension with your imagination, visualizing your in-breath surrounding the tension and your out-breath gently releasing it. Or, imagine the tension becoming warmer and melting away. Take as much time as needed. If any tense areas won't release, see if you can accept them as they are.

Next, bring your awareness to your breath for a few minutes or longer. Each time you become distracted, notice the distraction, and allow it to pass.

Then, silently ask yourself the question: *What is my motivation?* You may want to repeat it a number of times. Don't try to make anything happen; just see if an answer surfaces. If an answer doesn't become clear, simply sit with the question a bit longer. If an answer still doesn't come to you, you may want to try the meditation at a different time, or try a different technique, such as guided imagery or journaling, described next.

If an answer does come to you, gently rest your attention on your motivation for a short time, noticing your experience, including images, feelings, and physical sensations. Afterwards, writing down any insights will help you remember them.

2. GUIDED IMAGERY: WHAT DO I NOTICE?

In this technique, witnessing yourself as if you're looking at yourself from the outside can give you a different perspective and new insights.

Start by sitting up straight, without being rigid. Keep your spine aligned with your head and neck. Gently close your eyes. Try to release any physical tension, keeping your body relaxed but your mind alert.

See if you can allow just your spine to support you and the seat and ground to support you, and release any muscles not being used to support you right now. If any tense areas won't release, see if you can accept them as they are.

Next, bring your awareness to your breath for a few minutes or longer. Each time you become distracted, notice the distraction, and allow it to pass.

Now, witness yourself as if from afar. You could even imagine being an older, wiser version of yourself looking at your current self.

View yourself with eyes of compassion and understanding — and then see if you can tap into this sense of understanding. You may even want to ask the witness: *What is my motivation? How can I remain determined to make it happen?* If an answer becomes clear, write it down when you're finished with this practice.

3. RIGHT-HAND/LEFT-HAND JOURNALING

Journaling is an excellent tool for investigation. To use the right-hand/left-hand journaling practice, use your dominant hand to write a question, such as: *What is my motivation?* or *How can I remain determined?* Then answer the question with your non-dominant hand. The handwriting from your non-dominant hand may be hard to read, but should be legible enough for purposes of this exercise. The practice of writing with your non-dominant hand helps you tap into your subconscious, allowing you to discover inner wisdom.

VISUAL REMINDERS

Whether you've gained insight into your motivations — or not — choose a motivating factor that you'd like to work with. If you're not sure what motivates you, choose something tangible to get you started, such as a vacation or new car.

To help keep you determined to reach your goals, display a visual reminder of your motivation where you'll see it every day. For instance, a sales rep who wanted to land ten new customers a month used the number 10 as a screen-saver on her computer.

A sales rep who wanted a new Volvo displayed a picture of the car from the manufacturer's brochure and pasted his picture in the driver's seat window. Next to the car, he drew a thermometer and colored in a portion of it whenever he deposited money into his car account. This visual reminder helped him reach his goal.

Another sales rep realized that a need for achievement was her motivating factor. A tangible expression of that achievement was to pull her car into the Salesperson of the Month parking spot. Looking at the spot every day was her visual reminder. She became aware of negative self-talk, such as: *I won't make enough sales to be at the top*, and shifted to positive thoughts such as: *I easily exceed my quota and rise to the top*. She visualized herself pulling into the coveted space next to the front door of the building and within a few months, realized her goal.

Try this: Once you've identified your motivating factors, see if you can develop visualizations or affirmations to help reinforce them. Notice your thoughts and be mindful of any negative self-talk.

IT'S WHAT YOU DO THAT MATTERS

What are you going to do to spark your sales efforts and remain determined? Some days you might not feel like making your calls.

No matter how you feel, it's what you do that matters. Perhaps you can find some inspiration from the words of Henry David Thoreau, 19th century author, poet, and philosopher: *I can alter my life by altering my attitude. He who would have nothing to do with thorns must never attempt to gather flowers.*

A sales career isn't just filled with "flowers" — e.g., customers who always say *yes.* If that were the case, companies wouldn't need sales reps; they would only need order-takers. Thorns are part of the job.

I can think of times when I wanted to avoid the possibility of those thorns — times when it seemed as if my telephone and I were locked in a staring contest, sitting there for what felt like hours. But whenever such a time arose, I recalled my mentor's advice, with his voice echoing in my head: *How you feel is completely irrelevant. It's what you do that matters.* I picked up the phone and dialed.

ACTION PLAN

❋

EXERCISE
*Try one of the exercises in this chapter
to identify your motivating factors.*

EVALUATE
*Are the motivators you've identified working for
you, or is it time to identify new motivators?*

MOVING FORWARD
*How will you reinforce your motivating factors
going forward? Possibilities include:*

❋ Practicing a visualization using one or more of
your motivating factors.

❋ Creating affirmations that reinforce your motivating factors.

❋ Upon awakening in the morning, pausing to consider what motivates you before starting your day.

⁎ Continually reviewing and revising your motivating factors.

⁎ Finding a picture that inspires you and posting it by your desk.

⁎ Pasting your photo into a picture of a new car, vacation place, or any surrounding that motivates you.

⁎ Choosing one of your motivating factors and displaying a representation of it, such as a screen saver. For some, it might be as simple as posting a sign that says, "It's what you do that matters."

⁎

"True education can never be crammed and pumped from without; rather it must aid in bringing spontaneously to the surface the infinite hoards of wisdom within."

— Paramhansa Yogananda, 20th century guru

EPILOGUE

A N EPILOGUE GENERALLY describes what happens at the conclusion of a book.

What happens next is up to you. To ignite your sales power with Fuel, Air, and Spark, the next step is to practice — if only for a few minutes a day.

In the Appendix you'll find "18 Ways to Develop Your Power of Awareness," with suggested practices and blank space for your notes.

See if you can find one idea that resonates with you, and start with that one. Build from there. Try to create new ways of relating to your customers that can help boost your business. Like learning any new skill, repetition is key to your success.

Practicing these techniques and becoming more proficient using them will give you tools to navigate a path to the sale.

Consider this: The sales process is like building a bridge to cross the gap between you and your prospect or customer. It's not about forcing them to go in the direction you want; rather, it's about offering what makes sense to meet their needs. Maybe the gap between the two of you is so small that it's simple to navigate. Maybe the gap is so wide that there's no path to the sale. Building your power of awareness will help you know when to build a bridge — and help you understand which elements to use.

The Appendix offers suggestions for daily activities to help you build awareness. Remember that developing awareness can be practiced in a wide variety of ways. I hope you discover ways that will help you ignite your sales power!

※

APPENDIX

18 WAYS TO DEVELOP
YOUR POWER OF AWARENESS

Here are eighteen ideas for practices to try.

*You can try a new practice each day,
or skip around and choose those you like.*

*Note the ones that resonate with you and try
to integrate them into your sales activities.*

Notes

1. Meditate for two minutes at home.

Find a quiet place to meditate. (If you'd prefer to listen to a guided meditation, you can find a two minute meditation on www.joyrains.com.)

Sit in a comfortable position and lower your eyelids. Bring all your attention to your breath. Continue with the Simple Breath Meditation, as learned in Chapter 1.

Reflect: Were you able to focus on your breath during this meditation? This can be a challenging practice if you're new to meditation. Continued practice is key. How would you like to incorporate meditation into your life going forward? How often will you practice?

_____

_____

_____

_____

_____

_____

_____

_____

_____

Notes

2. Meditate for a few minutes before contacting a customer.

Find a quiet place to meditate. Sit in a comfortable position and lower your eyelids. Bring all your attention to your breath. Practice the Simple Breath Meditation as learned in Chapter 1.

After your meditation time, see if you can maintain present moment awareness as you meet with your customer. Any time your attention wanders, gently bring it back to your customer.

Reflect: How did the quality of your awareness affect your meeting? Do you want to continue to use this practice, and if so, how will you incorporate it into your sales activities?

_____

_____

_____

_____

_____

_____

_____

Notes

3. Treat your customer as your focal point during your meeting.

As you meet with your customer, direct all your attention to your customer, noticing words, voice inflections, rate of speech, and body language. Pay close attention to as many aspects of communication as possible.

Reflect: Were you able to keep your attention on your customer? Do you want to continue to use this practice, and if so, how will you incorporate it into your sales activities?

_____

_____

_____

_____

_____

_____

_____

_____

_____

_____

_____

Notes

4. Choose three affirmations and practice them first thing in the morning.

Choose three affirmations that resonate with you. Pick from the list of affirmations in Chapter 2, or create your own. Spend 5–10 minutes practicing them before you start your day, using the "Tips for Using Affirmations" guidelines in Chapter 2.

Reflect: Were you able to imagine what was described in the affirmations as if it was true? As you continue to use affirmations in the days and weeks ahead, notice any difference in your outcomes. Do you want to continue to use this practice, and if so, how will you incorporate it into your sales activities?

_____

_____

_____

_____

_____

_____

_____

_____

Notes

5. Spend five minutes visualizing an outcome you want.

Imagine as much detail as possible, envisioning the results as if they're already happening. The more specific, the better. The more senses you engage, the better.

Reflect: Were you able to imagine your outcome as if it was already happening? As you continue to use visualization in the days and weeks ahead, notice any difference in your outcomes. Do you want to continue to use this practice, and if so, how will you incorporate it into your sales activities?

_____

_____

_____

_____

_____

_____

_____

_____

_____

_____

Notes

6. *Practice a compassion meditation.*

Find a quiet place and choose a compassion meditation to practice for a few minutes or longer. You can find one in Chapter 4, search for one online, or create your own. As much as you can, try to tap into a feeling of caring and compassion for yourself and for others.

Reflect: Were you able to experience the feeling of compassion? Consider repeating a compassion meditation in the days and weeks ahead and note any changes in your outlook. Do you want to continue to use this practice, and if so, how will you incorporate it into your life?

_____

_____

_____

_____

_____

_____

_____

_____

_____

_____

Notes

7. *Visualize a goal.*

Take time to visualize a goal, imagining it to be real. Picture what you're doing and saying, what you're seeing and hearing, and how you're feeling. The more details you imagine and the more you imagine the goal as if it's true, the more effective your visualization will be. Post a visual reminder of your goal where you'll see it regularly.

Reflect: Were you able to imagine your goal as if it was already happening? Do you want to continue to use this practice, and if so, how will you incorporate it into your sales activities?

_____

_____

_____

_____

_____

_____

_____

_____

_____

_____

Notes

8. Create a dedicated meditation space at home.

A meditation space should include a dedicated place to sit, such as a chair or floor cushion, and could also include inspirational items, such as books of short readings (for before or after your practice), meditation beads, candles, or music. Try to set a regular time to mediate in this space, even for a few minutes a day.

Reflect: How do you envision yourself using the space you've created? How often will you use it?

_____

_____

_____

_____

_____

_____

_____

_____

_____

_____

_____

Notes

9. Meditate for five minutes at home.

Find a quiet place to meditate. Choose an anchor — a neutral object of awareness on which to focus your attention. Commonly used anchors are: your breath; your body; a word repeated silently, such as *peace*; sounds, such as ocean waves; or an object to hold, such as a smooth stone.

Sit in a comfortable position and lower your eyelids. Bring all your attention to your anchor. Continue with your meditation, using the guidelines in Chapter 1.

Reflect: How was your experience using your anchor during this meditation? Would you like to use the same anchor next time you practice, or try a different one? How will you incorporate meditation practice into your life?

_____

_____

_____

_____

_____

_____

_____

_____

Notes

10. Practice mindfully listening to a customer.

Concentrate on what your customer is saying. Try not to think about how you'll respond to your customer while he or she is speaking. Don't interrupt or finish your customer's sentences. Use silence when appropriate. More details on mindful listening can be found in Chapter 3.

Reflect: What was your experience using mindful listening skills? How will you use this practice going forward?

_____

_____

_____

_____

_____

_____

_____

_____

_____

_____

_____

_____

Notes

11. Tap into your unique motivational factors.

See if you can get clarity on what motivates you. Try meditating, using guided imagery, right-hand/left-hand journaling, or a different technique. See if you can find a visual reminder of one of your motivating factors.

Reflect: How will you remind yourself to tap into your motivation going forward?

_____

_____

_____

_____

_____

_____

_____

_____

_____

_____

_____

_____

_____

_____

Notes

12. Practice paraphrasing what you hear your customers say.

Either paraphrase your customers' words during your conversation — or paraphrase when your customers are finished explaining their needs, as described in Chapter 3.

Reflect: How was your experience using paraphrasing as a listening tool? How will you use this tool going forward?

_____

_____

_____

_____

_____

_____

_____

_____

_____

_____

_____

_____

_____

_____

Notes

13. Notice Your Stories

Do you want to change any stories you may be telling yourself? If so, note the methods you'll use to help establish new stories, for example, affirmations, visualizations, or posting visual reminders. Practice creating new stories using the methods you've identified.

Reflect: Have you noticed a shift in your thinking? Is this a technique you'd like to practice going forward, and if so, how will you continue to use it?

_____

_____

_____

_____

_____

_____

_____

_____

_____

_____

_____

_____

Notes

14. Record yourself saying affirmations.

Choose three to five affirmations from the list in Chapter 2, or create your own. Record yourself saying each affirmation ten times before recording the next one. You may want to pause between each repetition and leave enough space to repeat the affirmation aloud. You can also record your affirmations in first, second, and third person, for example, *I'm eager to make my prospecting calls; You are eager to make your prospecting calls; [Your name] is eager to make [his or her] prospecting calls.*

Reflect: How was your experience recording your affirmations? Did committing them to a recording help strengthen your belief in them?

_____

_____

_____

_____

_____

_____

_____

_____

Notes

15. *Listen to your recorded affirmations before bedtime.*

Sit or recline in a comfortable position and try to relax your body. Listen to your recorded affirmations, repeating each one aloud if desired.

Reflect: Is this a practice you'd like to continue in the days and weeks ahead? If so, what would be the best time for you to schedule this practice into your daily activities?

_____

_____

_____

_____

_____

_____

_____

_____

_____

_____

_____

_____

Notes

16. Practice using minimal encouragers.

Use *minimal encouragers* when listening to customers, whether talking to customers in person or on the phone. These are verbal and non-verbal responses that don't interrupt the speaker, as described in Chapter 3.

Reflect: How was your experience using this listening tool? Will you continue to use minimal encouragers in the future?

_____

_____

_____

_____

_____

_____

_____

_____

_____

_____

_____

_____

_____

_____

Notes

17. Practice compassion for a challenging customer or colleague.

Consider that harboring negative feelings toward someone else also affects you negatively. Choose one of the compassion meditations in Chapter 4, search for one online, or create your own. Find a quiet place and practice for a few minutes or longer.

Reflect: Were you able to feel compassion for a challenging person? How will you use this practice going forward?

_____

_____

_____

_____

_____

_____

_____

_____

_____

_____

_____

_____

Notes

18. Integrate mindful practices into your life.

You can practice being mindful almost anytime, anywhere. Consider integrating brief mindfulness breaks into your daily activities, such as pausing for a moment and noticing two full breaths; washing your hands and noticing the feeling of the soap and water on your skin; walking from one activity to the next, while bringing your attention to the soles of your feet as they connect with the ground.

Reflect: How was your experience of taking mindfulness breaks? Is this a practice you'd like to continue, and if so, how will you integrate mindfulness breaks into your daily routine?

_____

_____

_____

_____

_____

_____

_____

_____

A final thought …

In the Introduction, I shared my father's wisdom: *Sales is the worst paid job for those who don't work hard — and the best paid job for those who do!* Considering his words, I recommend that you work like a dog.

I happen to love dogs. I love the way dogs accept people for who they are, freely sharing their affection. When I gaze into their soulful eyes, I feel like they're totally present. A dog doesn't think: *Will I see FiFi in doggy day care tomorrow?* The dog's attention is fully in the present moment.

It's with this idea of complete presence that you can meet your customer. It gives the expression "work like a dog" a whole new meaning!

⁎

ACKNOWLEDGEMENTS

The support of my family and friends helped me transform the vision of this book into a reality. Thank you to: Bill for his steadfast belief in the value of the material and for encouraging me to write this book; Alli, for helping to sort through a mass of ideas and organize the text into its most salient points; Carrie, for pointing me to the Theory of Change and Logic Models and for an amazing eye for detail; Susan, for a consistent willingness to read numerous drafts and offer valuable feedback each time; Linda, for the ability to suggest small adjustments that made a big difference; and Deb, for offering her editorial expertise.

A special shout-out to Editor Barbara Kahl, who brought insight, precision, and dedication to this project. Also to Kaaren Christopherson, for a thorough and thoughtful review of the final manuscript. And finally, to David Moratto for the compelling book cover and interior design that has brought this manuscript to life.

Deep gratitude to you all.

www.ingramcontent.com/pod-product-compliance
Lightning Source LLC
Chambersburg PA
CBHW031943190326
41519CB00007B/632